Dark Days

& Other Poems

Andrew Aldred

chipmunkapublishing
the mental health publisher

Andrew Aldred

Published by
Chipmunkapublishing
United Kingdom

http://www.chipmunkapublishing.com

Copyright © Andrew Aldred 2014

ISBN   978-1-78382-076-4

Chipmunkapublishing gratefully acknowledge the support of Arts Council England.

About The Author

I have been in Mental Health Services since 1985, when I had a huge mental breakdown after serving in the Falklands with the army. Since then my life has been something of a rollercoaster of mental illness until meeting my wife Jane seven years ago.

I have been in and out of hospital from 1985 until 2009. I had an illness which I attributed to my father and resulted in me stabbing him in 1997 and going to the Edenfield Unit in Prestwich Hospital for 6 years. This is when I started to write poetry to keep myself sane and give me something to focus on.

Bite the Hand

I feel like a mischievous dog
That doesn't want to be nice
To the visitors
When they give me medication
It's all a big game
In this Toy town of a hospital
Carrot and stick, carrot and stick
Jumping through hoops
Why do they bother?
I don't know whether to laugh or cry
But I know I mustn't
Bite the hand

Pigeonholes

They want you to fit in a pigeonhole

They only see you in a box

That fits your exact description

My box is void

That is it's only description

I don't fit any category

Other than that of lunatic

Of all the boxes that are on offer

That is the best one

Sea of Bullshit

There's a lot of information around
With one common denominator
That is fear
A gigantic maze you are already trapped in
Your only choice
Is whether you believe in any facet of it?
Some people fake all their lives
Others find a rod for their backs
That beats them to death
All I have found is a sea of bullshit
I will eventually drown in

Why are they all so Angry

What is the point in getting drunk?

So you can have a pitch battle in the town centre

Every Friday and Saturday night

Do you like going to hospital

To be mended and stitched back together

Is there really nothing else in your life?

Join the army if you want to fight

I used to be able to go out and have a drink

Watch a band and have a laugh

But now it's oh so serious

If the football team loses they're looking for blood

Is that all that's important

Some people should get a life

Or stay indoors because I'll tell you what

They're not fit to be let out

You can send them all to prison for me

Don't go to Sleep

I wouldn't go to sleep tonight
When you wake up you'll get a fright
Your head will feel like a balloon
Your bowels will be out of tune
Your cock will feel like dropping off
And everyone will give you verbal when you get out of bed
What are these people about?
I wouldn't know if you told me

Religious Bigots

If a lot of you Christians
Knew more about Christianity
You would try to be more
Like Jesus Christ
All of you Muslims
Are too militant
To have any self control
And leave decent people alone
All of you Buddhists
Is too busy doing nothing?
To even try doing something you regret
In the first place
I don't want to change the world
I just think religion for the most part
Is a huge scam
And I want to be free to think that

Moderation

For ten years I have been trying
To live in moderation
Moderation in drinking and smoking
Moderate behavior in other ways
People have stretched me to the limit
And far beyond
I was known as a violent man
I seem to have to turn it around
Forever and a day
I was known as a rent boy
I'm going to find another way
To earn my pay
I was known as a soldier
Hardened by war
You'd better believe
I'm out of that now
And do you know
All I ever wanted to be
Was an average man on the street
I hope I'll see the day

Hardliners

All I see is hardliners and extremists
All over the news
Extremist Muslims, extremist Christians
Extremist policemen and extremist criminals
The rest of us are caught in the middle
Trying to survive
All the hardliners get sympathy
In jail, from the government and in the street
Because they have some ridiculous thing
They call a belief
And I'll tell you something else
They're all hypocrites
And even if they die for their beliefs
Things aren't that bad
That they'll be missed

Prostitute

They all love you

You like a bit of rough and tumble

In and out, give and take

Role reversal but it turns to fake

It all gets too much

They won't leave you alone

Drive you out of your home

You wanted to be a slave

End up with nothing

In a grave

One Michael Jackson

All everyone cares about these days is sex

There's one Michael Jackson and then there's the next

They're all so desperate for someone else's body

Tripping over themselves they're in such a hurry

Think nothing of abusing children

Hold their heads up in court

And they're so delighted when they win their case

Or get some weak slap on the wrist

It's almost as though they're unaware

The judge is a pervert and the whole case is fixed

In Charge

The person in charge
Always wants to assert their authority
By abusing it
They think their authority
Gives them a license to behave how they want
It's the same in every walk of life
The world would be better
Without authority

Religion

Religion is the basis of all bigotry
Pretending to be the answer to everything
It is the basis of all failure
A crux of corruption and greed
For its chosen few
A book of rules to read
Is something no one needs
Do you want to sow a poisoned seed?
And preach hatred to all and sundry
All you have to do is believe
In something with the substance of a cesspit
You can sell your soul to God
But he won't look after it
You can buy a place in heaven
But you won't get your money back

Full Circle

I've eaten shit
All my adult life
Has it ever crossed your mind?
That it could be you
That it might be unavoidable
The clock ticks
The pendulum swings
The bells chime
Cuckoo, cuckoo, cuckoo
It might be your turn
To eat a little humble pie
To live for some years
In a dark cesspit
Can you get on with it?

Boot Gang

You've seen them on television
With some group of burly thugs
Beating down a door
In five seconds flat
Going in with guns and batons
To catch you in your birthday suit
Guilty as sin
They'll turn you in
Good morning Britain
Have a good morning
And a few good years
In Her Majesty's Prison

The Ice Maiden

I never melted the ice maiden's heart
She sat in her chair a world apart
I showed her my poems one day
She said she thought they were very sad
Unfortunately I regarded this as a major achievement
And when one of her patients died
Through her overzealous use of medication
On his behalf I dared to say
That I heard his voice whilst having a bath
And he said he was better off dead
Needless to say she did not get the joke
And remained as frosty as the ice caps
Of a glacier surrounded by polar bears
Dear Doctor, was that a smile
Or just a change of expression on your face
Do you ever laugh when you go home?
Or just break down in tears

Set you up to Fail

They'll set you up to fail so many times
They want you to break down and cry
They want you to pay for your crimes
The traps are all laid years before
In some government book of torture
They want to break your spirit
To add your soul to their stature
You'll get wise to them
Will you be wise enough?
They can wait forever
Until they call your bluff
You're in their trap all the while
A whole world crawling with their servants
They want to bring you down
They want to make you worthless

Twisted and Broken

I'm twisted and broken
A dysfunctional mind
I fit into a society
Of a different kind
The symmetry is perfect
But it's bent out of shape
It makes perfect sense
But there's jagged holes that gape
It's out of your sight
But I can see it myself
It's plain to me
And nobody else
I'm secure in the knowledge
That I'm a damaged man
I'm criminally insane
And I know that I am
Twisted and broken
Bent out of shape
A character full of holes
That is lying agape

To be a Soldier

I remember the beatings
Being shouted at
Going to jail
Battle marches
Getting kit ready for use
The Sergeant Major used to tell us
There's plenty more outside
Waiting to be a soldier

Hopeless

What is there that I can do?
Spent the last four years in an RSU
Time in prison, record for violence
And schizophrenia to cap it all
Bi polar disorder, depression
Nerve palsy and a bad back
How can I get on the track?
My disability pension
Is all I've got?
Get a job?
I may as well fly to the moon
On a chocolate spaceship

Bullying Woman

She gives you the queues

And expects you to play the game

But you can bet your life

She won't play yours

She likes bullying men

But when she wants to be

She's a woman

Could probably drink me twice under the table

Boasts about eating chips and gravy

Like it's some big thing

She doesn't know

I've met her type before

But I'm still wondering

Why does she bother?

Demolition Forever

I sit in my room
And listen to the mechanical digger
And the grinding machine
Make hardcore out of rubble
I am used to it
It reassures me
And gives me a bit of interest
As I look out of the window
I am busy thinking
What will I do when they have built the site?

Pass Me By

I look at years gone by
Everyone passed me by
No one understood
When I sweated blood

I take drugs to kill the pain
I will not be the same again
Don't want to end up hating
Scared I will
Take that pill

There's no water in my well
I live in hell
Can't seem to reach out
But I have to
Can you?

Psychotic Illness

I was happy to face my own reality
Until the Social Services got hold of me
I could face the violence
I could stand being used
I thought I had a future
They stopped all of that

They wrapped me up in barbed wire
Gave me drugs so I could not see
Told me my reality was false
I had not done anyone any harm
Why all the alarm

Now it's a decade later on
My life for ten years had gone
They say I will need their drugs
For the rest of my life
And I am not sure which is worse
My reality or theirs
I wish I could have kept it to myself

Loss of Control

I am housebound
I don't go out
Paranoia broods
I cannot eat
And even if I could
I know all the food in my house is poisoned
I threw away the oranges I bought
For the good of my health
In the bin
And I might as well throw myself in too
Because I am desperate
Desperate to get out of this situation

Supermarket Horror

People are staring
Lights are glaring
Somehow I have to get
My groceries

I feel insecure
I cannot see properly
And if someone should say hello
I would probably die

Made it through the checkout
Got my vegetables
Out of the shop
And I realize
I have forgot one of my bags
And I have to go back
To the supermarket horror

The Cups

The cups line up to be filled with tea
Disheveled and odd in appearance
One in blue, another with flowers
Many not worthy of description
Some will find new homes
In patients' lockers
Others will be broken and thrown away
They will be taken, broken and lost
Until there are no more
And the staff will find us
Some of their well used relics

She's Winning

She must be over forty
At the very least
But still very attractive
Dyed ash-blonde hair
Long, with a perm
High heeled boots
Tight jeans
She's an eternal dolly bird
I hope she carries on
Until she's a glamorous grandmother
Twenty times over

Cheese and Onion

The smoke room stinks
Of cheese and onion crisps
There is nothing I can do
About the smell
It was there before I came
And will probably be there
Forever
Or at least until the next time
The decorators come
And even then
The smoke room will only smell of paint
For a short while

Whirling

The lunatic comes into the room
He asks for a light
Whirling and tense
You get the idea
He might lash out
At any moment
He smokes his cigarette
In double quick time
And goes out again
Whirling

Bad Girls

They strut around town in miniskirts
Larging it and chewing gum
After older men
You can see it in them
High heels, make up, cigarettes
All trying to outdo each other

Rap Music

Sex, horror, occult

It's all in today's music

More so than ever

People want to hear something sick

To see something that shocks

Drug culture and gangsters

Is the subject in rap music

With a generous slice of sex

People think it's big

To like their heroes

I used to

And I'm still interested

Cough Chorus

We have all staggered from out beds
It is early in the morning
And we are all trying to get our lighters
While the staff talk in the kitchen
About last drunken night
We will all be in the smoke room
Coughing up yesterday's dose of lung abuse
As though it's a competition
To see who can cough the loudest and most

Cigarette Man

He swears at the staff
In the hospital
As they try in vain to help
He gets a light for his cigarette
Off me
I like him
He is tall and thin
Like his Berkeley cigarettes

The Yellow Room

The yellow room is my sanctuary
I go there to play the guitar
Two or three times a day
And I am very rarely bothered
It is supposed to be an interview room
But I look on it as some sort of concession
To have the use of it

Living in a Vacuum

Sometimes I feel totally empty
Unfulfilled
As if someone had robbed me of my soul
I play guitar for hours every night
But no one listens
I wait for community leave
But it never arrives
I am supposed to be moving wards
But when?
It sometimes seems this system if designed
To make me feel hopeless
But people have the same situation to face
In the outside world
At the end of the day
It's a crazy existence
And we all have to survive
As best we can

Happy Smoke Room

People are happy in the smoke room tonight
We are all looking at each other grinning
And thinking what atrocities we would like to commit
To our friends under duress
It's like a pub with no beer
But plenty of drunks
This is a rehabilitation ward
And none of us will be here more than a year
Maybe that's why it's a happy smoke room

Westwood

It's Friday evening
And there's nothing to do
Except listen to the gangster rap show
I like the music
But these guys are thugs, pimps and drug dealers
Telling us about it
On radio one
If you're a gangster
At least you can listen to Westwood
On Friday and Saturday night
When you're in prison

The Army

I joined at sixteen

Anxious to fight and die

And be a hero

But after three years

Of working like a dog

I ended up in the Falklands

I was sick of the army

And I didn't feel I could go home

To a family that didn't understand

I had a mental breakdown

And fifteen years later

I'm still not the same

Manpower Services Commission

I went to Durham
To learn to be a gardener
But I couldn't even cope with that
I ended up drinking every night
And realized it was going nowhere
And to do anything
You had to really want to do it
And be satisfied with it
I quit

Working for the Council

I spent two weeks
Typing in a database
For a council office
It was unpaid
And the people very rarely talked
I felt like a spare part
My boss was never there
I needed three months in hospital
To get over the experience

Record Collector

I have been collecting records

For over twenty years

Shuffling through shelves of vinyl

In second hand shops

Searching for the elusive LP

I haven't seen for years

Usually I find something else

And the ones I want turn up

When I'm not looking for them

I usually come away with something new to listen to

Snoring

I lie awake at night
Listening to them snore
You can hardly believe
Five people can make such a din
Every hour I go for a cigarette
To make a clean break
So I can try and sleep
When I get back
But I know all I am in for
Is another hour of listening to them

Watch the World Fall Down

When Tony Blair and his cronies
Or whoever forms the next so called government
Makes society a damn sight worse
Than it already is
When nobody can smoke
When every second man is a War veteran
When nobody has a job
When half the world is in prison
I will laugh and say
I told you so
It's your mess
Go and clean it up

Old Habit

What will we do when there are no cigarettes?
And all our secret supplies have run out
Will we all live until we are ninety six?
And be a burden on society like that
Or switch to hard drugs
Or drink too much
We'll have to do something
We'll probably start smoking again
Nicotine is the single most useful drug
In our society
It causes no violence or crime
And relieves stress and tension
In this society that condones drug and alcohol misuse
Something is seriously wrong
When they have to do away with smoking

The Heterosexual March

They had a heterosexual march
Around Manchester today
Five people turned up
They thought about having a speech
And went to the pub instead
I saw someone campaign for smokers' rights
He smoked two cigarettes and went home
If you raise your voice these days
You'll get locked up
By some righteous set of bastards
Who think they represent society
Don't mention the silent majority

Intolerance

I don't want to know about the Ku Klux Klan

Any more that I want to know about the MOBOs

I'm not interested in dying for Allah

God and Buddha don't interest me either

I don't want to go to the toilet in a white zone

I just want a piss

I won't bother travelling out of my way

To drink in a pub full of gay people

And you all think you're so hard done to

You should try listening to yourselves

And I'll tell you something else

I'm not interested in the silent majority either

I won't watch television

I don't vote

You can have the world

But you won't own my soul

Have Your Pound of Flesh

The law can have its pound of flesh
It can have its cake and eat it again and again
Is it ever satisfied?
The answer is no
When there is nothing on the skeleton
It will move on to somebody else
Until there is nothing and no one left
Will it be satisfied then?
The answer is no
The law will never be satisfied

No Hope

You've got no hope
You're a single bloke
Nobody cares
They all despair
Of you and your ways

They want to freeze you out
Of what they're about
Cut you off
Hope you rot
When you go out you don't see a kind face

They want to go to your funeral
And say wasn't it a pity
He couldn't turn his life around
As they have a pint before they go to town
Hope you live to see them in the ground

Howling for Blood

They're a bunch of young men

Howling for blood

They'd run the country

If they could

They'll run you around

Kick sand in your face

It never enters their heads

That they're a disgrace

They all think they're so right

Think they can't lose a fight

When they do

They take the piss out of you when you're out of sight

They don't know

Before they leave they'll have to see the light

They're no better than anyone else

When you're on your own

You can't be Al Capone

Everyone is going to get screwed into the ground

And before you leave they'll turn you around

Die Trying

Get rich or die trying
It's the latest message
See them on television
Covered in cars and girls
While the record company boss
Smiles and spreads the word

I see you around
On the street and in town
Covered in gold
Wearing new clothes
But you can't afford a cup of coffee
Never mind the girls

You're selling the rich man's shit
But he's above the law
You think you're making money
Because you bought a second hand sports car
But you don't know the score
Spend your life in prison
On the wrong side of the law

Disabled Man

I've got to go out today
Soon I'll have to earn some pay
I'd feel better about it
If I had a gun pointed at my head
But I'd better get on with it
Because no one else is going to give a shit
About me and my problems

I'm only forty years old
Spent half my life working
Trying to get a job
People don't understand
That I'm severely ill
I look healthy enough
Never knew life would be so tough

If you're disabled
Don't ride your luck
Don't just draw your benefits
And be a lame duck
No one gives a damn
You'll end up out of luck
And in the can
That's what it's like for a disabled man

I Took a Wrong Turn

It was about twelve years ago
I think I recall
I got kicked down the stairs
But I didn't fall

I took a wrong turn
And walked ten miles on
Before I realized
I was in a different town

I'd been drinking all day
With some Irish folk
I got to their house
And got kicked out without my coat

Thank God they hadn't taken
My credit card and wallet as well
They'd just removed
Some money from it

Dark Days

I caught a taxi home
From a kebab shop
He charged triple rate
And ripped me off

If you had to ask me
About the last twenty years
And where it went wrong
All I could say was I took a wrong turn

My God

My God is a little man
He sits on a fluffy cloud
With his dog
The kettle is never off the boil
He has a piano
And a clock that chimes every hour
He never worries
No one ever calls to see him
He watches us from a distance
And he is more contented than anyone

Imagining Freedom

What will it be like?

Will I fall flat on my face?

Spend my life in the pub

And lose the race

Will I turn to drugs?

Or be perpetually ill

Will I be able to cope with?

So much time to kill

Could I keep myself fed?

Be able to see the Doctor on time

And keep my head

What will it be like?

Will I fall flat on my face?

Or be able to rejoin

The human race

Poor Jesus

Poor Jesus had a miserable life
And a miserable death
He was a very decent fellow
But people had to corrupt his memory
By passing their sins on to him
I think he should be remembered
As the figurehead of Christianity
And not as a rubbish tip
For the sins of unworthy people
Who have not got the strength of character
To deal with or take responsibility
For their own sins

Time for Myself

I will have time for myself
To feel as miserable as I like
And to do very little
I want to rest and relax
I don't want to be bothered
With anyone or anything
I want to cut off and drift
I am going to be a nomad again
Keep the fold for yourselves
My place is not with you
Even when I am in the pen
I am alone

Wrong

The thing about the people in charge
Is they never get it right
They get it wrong and wrong again
They never get it right
They think the way to fix your head
Is take a hammer to your brain
They never seem to realize
That they are plainly insane
Good luck on your trip to nowhere
Give yourself a pay rise
Have another piece of cake
You're someone I despise

Tutankhamen's Tomb

You're looking for me in my room
I seem to be in bed
But I'm in Tutankhamen's tomb
You see me sitting in my chair
You're looking at me
But I'm not there
I'm sailing on a lost ship
In a forgotten sea
Alone and without company
I'm a needle in a haystack
That's ten miles square
A shadow in the night
That isn't there
And when you find me
I will be somewhere else
Beyond the reach of God
And the Devil himself

Andrew Aldred

The Home Office

I went to the Home Office
To take a look
There were fifty million pigeon holes
And a case full of books
She said Mr Aldred take a seat
We'll find a pigeon hole
Where you can fit
I sat on the floor
For half an hour
My brain fell out
And she trod in it

Stuck with Yourself

You can take a load of drugs
Or get a book off the shelf
You can go to the pub and get drunk
Or ask the Doctor for help
You can pray to God to change
Or pray to the Devil himself
Be a sycophant and try to please
A dictator or somebody else
But after you've been everything
That you can possibly be
And there is nothing else
There's the real you and the real me
And we're stuck on our own
With ourselves

Think of Them

They've stripped my soul
My life is so bare
An empty heart
A mind full of despair
But I'll put it all in perspective
For you and your God
In the paper today
A child was killed by a dog
You might have it worse than me
But if you would only see
While you are drawing your breath
Children in Africa
Are starving to death
So my life is a total wreck
And I fear for my health
I'll never turn my back
On life itself

Psychopaths Without Diagnosis

You can see it in their manner

You can see it in their gait

Peculiar mannerisms

Minds that hate

They're locked in a Wendy house

They can do what they like

It's a holiday camp

That might as well be a spike

They are all sons and daughters of want

They can't be happy with what they have

There's no joy in their lives

It's funny but it's not a laugh

Their crimes aren't serious

They don't get noticed

They are psychopaths

Without diagnosis

Numb

I used to drink all night
So I could cry myself blind
I used to feel the pain
Of going out of my mind
I used to have some innocence
Some things that were nice
I know I'm very lucky
To have any sort of life
I wish I could care more
About the world and myself
I'd be intelligent
If I wasn't so dumb
I know all I am
Is numb

Silver Bracelet

She came in my room
And loved me one night
There were two sides to her
A wrong and a right
All there is in a woman
Is the worst and the best
After that
There's nothing else
I might fall in love again
Or save myself the grief
I gave her something
A sort of charm
A silver bracelet
To wear on her arm

Legoland

The children are twisted and psychopathic
They drive themselves berserk
They try to build a structure
But they have the co- ordination of spastics
They don't know what it is
They are trying to build
I'm just sat here
Detached from the reality
That they are trying to manipulate
They haven't realized
That they will never win
The institution they are in
Knows them and their tricks
And dreams of new traps for them
Before they have got out of
The ones they are in

Longer than Natural Life

So you want to be the man

Who runs this place

They talk behind your back

But not to your face

You sell the drugs

You run the game

At the end of the day

It's all the same

Whether it's the law or your own

You end up to blame

A bullet in the head

Or a blow with a knife

Or at best locked up

For longer than natural life

Drowning

You want me to save you
From drowning
But I'm drowning myself
And you're pulling me in
We all have our own seas of despair
There are never enough lifeboats around
Too many sinking ships
And we all eventually drown
I'll keep you afloat
For as long as I can
It's just a hard fact of life
When it all hits the fan
I'll have to let go
When I've carried you all I can

Free

I wish I could be free

From Jesus, Mohammed and the Mental Health Service

There are a whole lot of people

This world could do without

Fighting it out on the streets

They all want to claim your soul

As theirs and theirs alone

I have a temple inside my head

A place that is sacred to me alone

I live there alone

I could tell you about it

But you wouldn't understand

I think you should build something

Of your own

And forget about the rest of them

If they're Stupid Enough

There's a whole lot of people
That think they're in charge
I don't know what they're doing
Let loose and at large
They all think they own you
That you're there to please them
So if someone is stupid
Ignorant and large
If they're stupid enough
Put them in charge

Bunch of Ravers

I'm living with a bunch of ravers
I'm sure they're trying to save us
But I don't know what from
Is reality that grim
Does it exist at all
I only see things
That are real to me
I'll let the rest of the world get on
With living in a berserk spaceship
It's not that I don't give a shit
Maybe it's that we had something better
When I was a kid
I'm sure I'd work it out
If I wasn't busy
Trying to relax

Is Everyone Mad

I'm mad and I'm the first to admit it
But I'm sure everyone else is
And if you're all saying you're sane
What the hell are you doing
Living in a mental hospital
The staff, well
Most of them can't do anything else
So they're reduced to coming in
To tell a bunch of lunatics what to do
And the hospital staggers along
Like the catastrophe it is
I think I'll just opt out
I don't belong here
So I won't be there anyway

Day of Miracles

They gave you a day of miracles
To keep you alive
Pin your hopes on it
But it never arrives
So we're all growing older
And closer to death
They want you to repent
And draw your last breath
Well, don't be sorry
This life is all anyone has
And you all think it is a living death
I'm telling you all you'll be dead soon enough
Don't you call the hangman's bluff
You'd better make the most of it
Because it's all there is
And all there'll ever be
And soon it'll be someone else
Instead of you and me

Clinically Dead

I look at my head
In the mirror
And pull a face
The features move
Of who it was
There's still a trace
I spend a lot of time
Trying to convince myself
Life isn't a joke
Things really matter
And there is some hope
But I'm beyond redemption
In my own head
I seem to be alive
But I'm clinically dead

Tricksters and Fakes

Here we are on another jolly japes
With another set of tricksters and fakes
Implying things they don't even know
Trying to make you wither while they grow
Everything they do is behind your back
They'd love to give you a heart attack
It's all right saying they don't know what they do
But I'm not Jesus and neither are you
So come out of hiding
I don't like your tricks
Show us what you're made of
But don't step in it

Friend of Misery

There was a time
When my only delight
Was my friend of misery
Through the night
Getting off on my woes
Solves the situation
Until the problem goes
When I see or hear
Someone sadder than me
I'm overjoyed and laughing
Not many people can see
How sad it gets
When your only joys
Are worries and frets

Control

A series of corrupt societies
Based on perverse practices
Extreme corruption and power
Interlinked and tightly sealed
Are in control of this
And every other country
What is the point of it all
The people at the top choke
On their own vomit and greed
They are busy slaughtering themselves
Because they don't know what else to do
Someone has to run the country
I'm glad it's not me
What is the solution?
I can't think of one

Ghost

I'm a ghost of someone
You used to know
There's a secret
That isn't there
Locked in my soul
There's a whole lot of things
That you don't understand
I'm similar
But I'm a different man
All you are is a memory
But I'm not sure you're there
I'm chained up and surrounded
But I'm not sure I care

Broken Brain

I saw a film today

About a young man

With a broken brain

Who tried to live his life

By his diaries and journals

Until he realized

It wasn't worth it

I let my memories ruin me for a while

Flashbacks of madness, confusion and misery

I realized I had to start again

Like the young man

Throwing his journals and diaries into the bin

And setting fire to them

You can't live in the past

If it is destroying you

It's a waste of time

You have to move on

Start a new life

And try to keep your head above water

Rather be on Mars

There are eleven people here
That I've run out of things to say to
Some of them believe in taking drugs
Some of them don't believe in anything
I'm trying to get some work
Having a relationship with my girlfriend
Trying to move on from this dump
And I'm not getting listened to
Or so it seems
It's very frustrating indeed
I come back to a sea of empty faces
Have to leave my girlfriend in bed
And believe you me
Rather than come back here a night
I would wish myself in outer space
You guessed it
I'd rather be on Mars

Have You Seen the Light?

It's a question I have been asked a lot of times
Have you seen the light?
Do you know the truth?
Do you want us to crucify you one more time?
Some people are like Jesus Christ
They go straight ahead and bite the bullet
Others are like me and digress
Buy a bit more time and see a situation out
It's alright being without sin and dying honorably
But you're not going to be able to enjoy it afterwards
So they're all praying to Jesus in Church on Sunday
Wanting to be like his perfect example
To die for any reasonable excuse
In the name of King, country and religion
I'll ask you whether you have seen the light
Jesus was hung on a cross two thousand years ago
When he was dead his corpse rotted
And now there's nothing left of it
He'll be remembered forever but his life was cut short
I'm not Jesus Christ by any means but I have seen the light

Police Assault

The policeman notices she's had a bit to drink
He makes a rude remark as she passes by
Like a fool she bothers to give him an answer
And he creates a situation
Where he can pressurize her into a reaction
And he and his colleagues can jump on her
Two minutes later she's in a headlock
Held on the floor by a woman constable
Telling her not to make things worse for herself
Than they already are
The van will be coming around any minute
And they'll put her with the rest of them
In their new purpose built police station
Where they'll extract their ounce of flesh
And whatever else they can
Before they let her go
And she's another one that will be saying
Those boys in blue
They're a set of bastards

Con Trick

They're selling Jesus' heads in gold and jewels
For extortionate amounts of money
My gold cross is bigger than yours mate
I'm a personal friend of the Deli Lama
And I spent thirty one million pounds of Kabala
And doesn't it make you sick
What the stars waste their money on
What about the starving millions
But there's nothing in that for the stars
It's not hip and it doesn't sell
All they want is the influence the church gives them
They're buying into society
They're buying an image and some influence over people
When religion is corrupt from the top down
What hope is there for anyone?
Jesus saves and the church has a big bank balance
It's all about money and nothing else
The church is the biggest landowner in Great Britain
God is very rich
And millions are starving in Africa

The Mentally Ill Health Service

This is an institution that doesn't care
It wants to walk all over you
It wants to make you ill
They don't want to help you
They want you to be mentally ill
To keep their hostels and hospitals full
And once you are there
They want you to stay there and keep quiet
Whilst they walk all over you
A lot of the people in this profession
Are more mentally ill than the patients
And twice as dangerous
They are always there when you don't want them
They like to keep you annoyed
It satisfies their cravings
A reaction justifies their existence
They feed off it
This is a sick institution
And when you need them they are on holiday

Ministry of Injustice

They like to look down their noses at you
They earn more in a year than I will in a lifetime
Through other people's misfortune
If it was up to me
I'd make them all dig a tunnel
Underneath the Atlantic Ocean to America
With picks and shovels
So they would know what work was
Their punishment for working in a filthy profession
The rich and famous get let off
So do the worst criminals
Because they've got the money
To buy their freedom and receive a token punishment
The law is an ass
Because it is as stubborn as hell
And it has to be seen to be right
They want you to surrender your soul
Bow your head and eat shit
They're just as guilty as the criminals
But they're out there driving sports cars
And getting up to all sorts of mischief

Middle Aged

There comes a time
When you have done most of the things you wanted to do
And you are too tired to reach out to do anything else
You can't really change direction
And you have found the facets that make up your character
You may have found the right partner
And made a bit of money
You are contented for the first time in your life
But you always have to cope with the fear
What happens if something goes wrong?
How will you ever build something else?
You have found a pigeon hole you can fit in
You have got your dream
What if they take it away from you?
When you have nothing to lose it doesn't' matter
When you have fought all your life to get somewhere
And that is all you are ever likely to have
And all you ever wanted
There is only one way
You have climbed your mountain
You have to go downhill

Broken Home Office

Now they call themselves the Ministry of Justice

These set of bureaucrats somewhere in London

Who hold me in their power

They always got around to my case too late

If they can't handle their workload

Why are they in charge of anything?

A prominent politician has recently said

They need to be totally reorganized

Modernized and made more efficient

It has all been ignored

All they have is a new name

Their decisions are irrational and inconsistent

What they do makes very little sense

In that in two similar instances

They do two different things

They are not about fairness and equality

Or justice for that matter

They are a set of people

Kicking me around from pillar to post

For no good reason

Apart from the fact that they can

Tracks, Rope or Drugs

It's such an awful shame
Their friends couldn't say the right words
Their family couldn't help them
The Doctor couldn't mend what was broken inside
They were so alive and so successful
They had it all but they could not admit defeat
So they had to kill themselves
To avoid embarrassment and failure
They had seen enough in their short life
And couldn't cope with any more
They had become hideous to themselves
Like a piece of antique furniture
Destroyed in a frenzy with an axe
They had been hanging on the brink for a while
Dabbling in things they shouldn't do
Then they snapped and became another suicide
They swam too far out to sea
And got washed up on the beach
It could have been anyone

Militant Social Worker

The militant social worker called today
And got me out of bed
Her face was gaunt and drawn
And her hair badly dyed
She was determined not to like me
And to cut me down to size
She announced herself to be my connection
With the home office
Of whom she was a servant
She did not want to know anything about me
And obviously had not read any reports
Before she saw me
And she wanted to make decisions about my life for me
I tried to be nice to her
When I realized it was pointless to argue
I wish these people had standard procedures and ethics
And personalities did not come to bear so much
What is the point in having a psychopath
As a social worker
She should be serving time in Broadmoor
For having a personality disorder

Climate Change

The seasons are lopsided
Winter comes later than it used to
Summer comes towards August and September
There's heavy rains in Britain now
Floods every year
When will we all start to care
About global warming
Whenever it is it seems it will be too late
This isn't some Hollywood movie
With a happy ending
This is a planet starved of oxygen
Trying to put itself to right
We're killing ourselves to live
We can't make the sacrifice required
We want cars and planes and nuclear bombs
We want more children than we can support
We are all prepared to ruin things
In the name of our own greed
We want to destroy everything
In the name of evolution

The Tip of the Iceberg

Sometimes something stands out at you in the news
Something repulsive or astonishing in some sense
It either stinks to heaven or it's very frightening
New solar systems created by man
Or some child disappearing never to be seen again
It's only what they want you to see
There's a lot more going on and a lot of pointers
That all lead to the human race getting too clever
Too big for it's boots by a long chalk
Whether it's Dolly the sheep or the next neutron bomb
It's the tip of the iceberg and the shape of things to come
Is there room for a normal life for anyone
It's the tip of the iceberg we're all frozen in
When we should be living normal lives
We might need more than global warming to be free
Of the incarceration and helplessness we're all trapped in

Convince the Doctor

He comes here made of granite
He has the manner of a Scottish gangster
And he probably has a shotgun or three
I've seen his car with its personalized number plate
And I'm sure the home office thinks he's great
He's not in the habit of giving anything very much
He lacks what people call the human touch
He's more skeptical than anyone I've ever met
Getting one over on him is something you're not likely to get
He's a staunch disciplinarian
And he doesn't like mistakes like me
He's in this business to condemn the mentally ill
His patients are condemned to listening to him every week
When he's not on holiday or on annual leave
Being anything mundane wouldn't enter his head
I've even called him a psychopath
I doubt he finds anything about himself very amusing
Apart from the fact that he disagrees with everything
And that the mentally ill should be locked away forever

Pray for Batman

They locked me up ten years ago
And passed me down the system
Pitifully slowly and painfully
I had everything going my way
And then is all fell to pieces
My girlfriend got ill
We turned to alcohol for help
The building where I lived kicked me out
And now I'm on the acute ward
Taking a passing interest in the Batman film
As I walk past the television
The Doctor and the Social Worker hate me
The nursing staff can't move me on
I'm sure the Home Office is mad
I'll pray to Batman because I might as well
God, where are you now

The Shining Example

The shining example is placed on the wall
Let it be a shining example to us all
The patient who is supposedly well
And the Doctor who looks like a devil from hell
So you think this patient can tell us at twenty five
How we should live and be alive
You think this shining example on the wall
Is a shining example to us all
Well I've been sober and more often drunk
Fought in two wars and driven a tank
Tried for years to get a job
To live a good life and evade the mob
I've been locked up in worse places for years
I've had treatment that has reduced me to tears
I'm disabled in my back and both legs
And I really wish I could be someone else
But they'll never let me be right about anything
I've got to lose because they won't let me win

Tony Blair's stolen My Cigarettes

I went to the houses of parliament

To make my point

I sat there for hours

And went for a pint

I went to the gents

And felt in my coat

I was thinking that I

Could do with a smoke

I found my lighter and my keys

But no cigarettes

I pressed the alarm bell

And wondered what to do next

I went back to the bar

Feeling worried and vexed

And there he was with a tin of ready rubbed

I said I am going to smoke in this pub

Go to the off licence and get me some cigarettes

He said, "Have one of yours."

"I stole them myself."

I said, "Tony, you're a bastard."

And bought him a pint

Saddam Hussein's Death

Think of what they did to Jesus Christ
Then have a look at Saddam Hussein's life
They're two different people
With a similar end
Both executed and condemned
A politician complained about it
Others said nothing
It's happened to plenty of innocents
He didn't complain about them
Is it really some sort of stand?
Against the death penalty
Or some cynical publicity stunt
George Bush used to execute them
In droves every day
They won't complain about him
Or will they?

Failure of Gangster Culture

So they offered you a job in a factory
They want you to press jeans for them
But you'd rather be prostitutes
They offered your boyfriend a job
They wanted him to work in a garage forecourt
Cleaning cars and driving them around
But he'd rather sell drugs
What are you going to do?
When you've been to prison and got out
When the law is watching you
To see what you are up to
The choice is yours
And the circles get smaller
When are you going to get a job?
When will you work in a factory?
Unfortunately you're a waste of time
You've been sold the wrong aspirations
On the television music channel

My Friend

My friend moved the other day
To a worse ward in a secure hospital
It will set him back some more
He's in a situation he can't acknowledge
He says he can't repent
And he can't get on with it
He's been a good friend
But you don't get anything for quitting
Only a worse situation than you had before
He wants achievement and privilege
But you don't get that for nothing
He's a talented man with a lot to offer
But they're busy reducing him to nothing
He won't take what's on offer
It's not good enough for him
I have to stand by and let it happen
It's a shame and such a waste

Softens the Blow

I've taken up watching television recently
Too bad I didn't do it before
It makes it easier to cope with real life
I've seen incest on Eastenders
Gangsters, pimps, prostitutes, politicians
Corrupt men of the cloth
And corrupt everyone else
And it seems to me to be very like real life
It gets my own life into perspective
I'm staying out of the pubs and out of trouble
Watching television at my girlfriend's house
Getting an education that I'm not the only one out there
And if I see something bad happen
Or something bad happens to me
Or my family or someone I know
Watching television will help soften the blow

Corporal Punishment

I remember someone saying
This will hurt me more than it hurts you
The sadistic sod
Hitting a child with a fist or a rod
People who put themselves above everyone else
Who mistakenly believe there's a need for them?
It can get so bad
But where does it stop
The victim ties a rope around themselves
And takes a drop
Or gets beaten to a pulp
Or viciously raped
Because they won't give in
To a person that hates
The majority can only hope
That civilisation will get better
And people obey the law to the letter
Every day it's something we hear in the news
Another poor person being hurt or abused

Dead Soldier

He laid down his life

He took all he could take

He left a wife and three children

Crying at his wake

He'd become a Queen's sergeant aged twenty four

Little did he know he'd be going to war?

It had all been so easy

He'd been such a success

Two sons and a daughter

And a wife in distress

Their daddy's life for his country

He died a hero for us all

He should have been a sales assistant

In a shopping mall

He wanted death or glory

He ended up with both

They cried their eyes out

At his funeral toast

Dark Terraced Street

There are some trees at the end of the street
That cast a shadow over the area
As well as a disused church
With hardly an intact pane of glass
There's a cripple that feeds the pigeons
At the same time every day
There's a collection of cars
Lurking around the way to the main street
Parked there while their owners
Go about their dubious business
The alleys are full of rubbish
Broken fridges and rubble
There's a thriving school at the other end of the street
But we never see the children
Although sometimes we hear them
There's not much sunshine on Sunning hill Street
When it's the middle of winter

The World outside the Window

The hospital I am in
Looks out on a school at the back
There's some rough land
And a house next door
To the garden shed
I have noticed the sunsets
As I look down the valley
Aeroplanes leaving white lines in the sky
The birds singing in the morning
And the children playing in the fields
I think of my situation
My girlfriend on the other side of town
Everything I have done with my life
And I know things are alright
There is a God for me
I am at peace with myself
And the world outside the window

Bad Weather

It's pouring down outside
Sometimes it's freezing
We couldn't go out last night
So we got drunk at home
Everyone's getting nowhere fast
And it's all so depressing
I only hope Christmas will get better
I held out some sort of hope
For a better life on my discharge
And it is better in some ways
At least I am relaxed
And I can cope with my life
No more over excitement and madness
No extremes of mood
No paranoia and psychosis
Just depression and bad weather
Another bleak winter to get through

Acceptance

My time is nearly done
Ten years of aggravation
My life is in a different situation
Thank God it's one I can gratefully accept
Not one I am desperate to reject
I can be happy like everyone else
And happier than most
Is it just that I am recovering from my illness?
Or that I've got a girlfriend that I love
Or is it that I rarely see my parents
And I can get on by myself
These are all facets in making me well
The nightmare is all but over
What was it all about?
Was it just an illness?
I don't even want to know
I need to embrace a new and better life
Pity I've had to wait nearly forty years for it
I'm fed up with thinking about it

Work Until You Drop

I've got an army pension
I'm better off than most
I only work for an occupation
You might think that's ideal
But it makes me really sick
When I see some pampered movie star
On television in a helicopter
Turning up at a nightclub
That's not work
They're not worth that
May I remind you?
They've risen the retirement age to seventy
You're still expected to contribute
When you're arthritic and you're heart is weak
So some pipsqueak can drive around in a Bentley
And drink champagne
At two hundred and fifty pounds
For every bottle
Work until you drop
See them on television and vomit

Evolution

Life moves so fast these days
They've got to invent the latest thing
Just to get paid
Records replaced by CD's
Walkman's by MP3's
There's IPOD's and mobile phones
That does everything apart from change your bed
I wish I could buy something and keep it
For more than two years
Before it gets out of date
Spare parts are impossible to get
Apart from on the internet
You might as well buy brand new
You can't save much by buying second hand
They'll just sell you something incomplete and obsolete
For ten pounds less
So I can't keep what I've got for five minutes
Because the managing director has to drive a Jaguar
It's all false economy
And it's them taking my money

They Took the Chairs

They took the chairs out of the smoke room today
Part of the latest purge
This time it's on smoking
When will they be happy?
Why can't they leave us alone?
What is it all for?
It's not for the good of me or my health
It's not good to smoke
But it's better than being miserable and anxious
No one is happy
Why do we bother?
I am upset and I have told them why
They are upset because they have had to listen to me
It all comes from having people in charge
Who is brain dead?
And out of touch with reality
Like fools we follow their orders
Where will it all ends

The Capitalist Society

The capitalist society
Preys on the weak and the poor
It finds them places to live
So it can abuse them
Housing associations, mental hospitals
They're all on the make
They'll put you in their spike
So they can get their money's worth
Of whatever you have got
They don't want you to have an education
Even if you get one
They'll make it null
All they want to do
Is pillage and rape everything you've got
When they get old, weak and poor
The same thing happens to them
This is what society's promoting
It scarcely stops short of cannibalism

Bad Feelings

All these feelings of being raped and abused
I wish I could get them out of my system
The fear and paranoia every time I sleep
The suspicion of the company I keep
It's all been a snowball
With me inside it
Blown up out of all proportion
Until I believed my own bullshit
But was it really that
There's always some doubt in my mind
Feelings that have run very deep
The fact that I committed a serious crime
Inside of this illness
I've got to keep a balanced mind
And not get poisoned by bad feelings
And not get poisoned

www.ingramcontent.com/pod-product-compliance
Lightning Source LLC
Chambersburg PA
CBHW031214270326
41931CB00006B/559